The
Out-Islands

The Out-Islands

Martin Edwards

Smokestack Books
1 Lake Terrace, Grewelthorpe,
Ripon HG4 3BU
e-mail: info@smokestack-books.co.uk
www.smokestack-books.co.uk

Poems copyright
Martin Edwards, 2021,
all rights reserved.

ISBN 9781916312166

Smokestack Books
is represented by
Inpress Ltd

*It's a strange courage
you give me ancient star.*

*Shine alone in the sunrise
to which you lend no part.*

William Carlos Williams

for Kate, Keir and Isaac

Contents

Songs	11
birthmarks	12
Labour	13
Whistle	14
Paperwork	15
Moonlanding: Wales 1969	16
A Family	17
fog	18
Boats	19
mute	20
lunar	21
Swimming	22
coastal	23
Citizen	24
Bournemouth	25
Antarctica	26
Robin	27
rainstorm with goldfish	28
beach road	29
Surfer in Autumn	30
The Spiders	31
breaking the silence	32
morning song	33
Cows	34
Dying Dog	35
Near the Pole	36
Bunuel's Unmade Film	37
Book with ants and a fly	38
Car Wash	39
Second Hand Cadillac	40
Shanty Town	41
Ex-Patriots	42
On the Shining Path	43
Oxford Town	44
Freetown	45
undertow	46
driving in snow	47

kate's feet	48
whales	49
taking a bath	50
Party	51
Child	52
Definitions	53
The Lecture	54
The Neon Party	56
Lullaby	57
The Possibility of Snow	58
Hate	59
Leveret	60
Conjuring Rowena	61
Grand Canyon	63
Delinquents	65
Frank O'Hara's Collected Poems	66
Homesick Blues	67
Grandfather/Clock	68
Erosion	70
Unreal!	71
Saint Martin	73
Something	74
Nativity	75
Mother to Child	76
The Great Umbrella	77
Leeks	78
Undertakers	79
grief	80
West Ogwell Church Devon, March 2019	81
I promise you	82
sweeping the monastery porch cittaviveka	83
Ash	84
Allotment	85
River in the Woods	86
balcony	87
The Rest of My Life	88
In 1989	90
White Moths	91
Acknowledgements	92

Songs

When our hearts were like tulips
our fathers sang
The Riddle Song
and *Aunt Rhody*
and dark hairs grew
through our pale skin

our fathers sang
Careless Love and
Hard Rain
teaching us not to be
too kind

in the pines in the pines
where the sun never shines
our long feet sprung for journeys

birthmarks

on my shoulder a splash
of moon-bleached skin

a blemish on soft
flesh below an eye

and these sour little scars
on thigh and knee

where brake lever
and modeling knife

went in

Labour

Dad balancing my placenta,
on top of the coals.
It's wrapped in a page
of *The Manchester Guardian*.

The soggy parcel blots the flames,
its stubborn strap-line:
Bevan Dead.

But he fans them alive
with a classical E.P.
(He's a young man meaning
to get somewhere.)

And now he's listening intently
at the foot of the stairs.
The midwife grins
over the banisters.

And there is a not unpleasant smell
of cooking blood
as he takes her advice
and strolls,

away from me,
out into cool, September air.

Whistle

Dad showing me how to whistle
using a blade of grass.

Listen, he says,
Now you try.

And I learn how precise
the word blade is

blooding my lips
on its edge.

Paperwork

Leaving for Australia in a couple of days,
Dad opening a drawer

to show me wills and deeds,
insurance and pensions

all the paperwork
of a life in order.

≈

Outside Oxford a hot air balloon
floats up from the palm of England

and I imagine him looking down
tiny spectacles in a tiny window

at the Pacific's vast origami
folding and unfolding

suggesting this and that
some land, a runway,

anywhere.

Moonlanding: Wales 1969

for Michael Collins

It was the summer of my first camera
and the first footprint on the moon.

I felt sorry for the man who
stayed in orbit,

competent, correct,
whom no one remembers.

That's me
looking down

through the porthole of this photo
at my mum, so young and afloat

in the middle of a step
and my handsome dad, about to speak,

to unfold
the never-to-be-disturbed,

weightless
dragon-flag of his tongue.

A Family

The mother's frying a paste of spices:
turmeric, fenugreek, coriander and cumin,
talking about a journey to Spain.

While the father retreats
into his garden,
deeper and deeper every year.

You know little of them
(absorbed by childhood
while they were young

and absent later).
You call out, *Mother!* *Father!*
and wait and wait for the words to return

like children
at dusk, stained
with spices and gardens.

fog

(*Southend*)

fogs
    erase
        an estuary

setting the boats
            afloat
                in space

then sinking them
            completely

until

the tentative
        half-choked
                cough

of a cockling boat

articulates
    a wake
        that's wide enough

to pleat
    the whiteness
             the length of the beach

and set
    the silence
        slapping

Boats

I listened to his voice on the shortwave radio,
almost lost in the Roaring Forties:
It's blowing a gale here... over.
discovered again in the calm of the Sargasso Sea:
I love you both...
then glowing with sun from the Caribbean,
frosted and scared as he rounded the Horn
to gaze for the first time on the Pacific Ocean,
quoting us Keats and describing
a nasty cut on his thumb.

How can I forget him,
out in the garage every weekend,
working on the boat,
the Morris displaced,
the varnish on its wooden trimmings peeling?

How can I forget the start of the race:
the garage demolished,
due to a miscalculation
of the relative widths of boat and door
and then out in the bay so many boats
each moving at a different angle to the wind?

And his voice on the radio and then
nothing, and nothing.

Stories in the papers for a couple of days,
my mother interviewed
and the boat at last found
dragging its anchor off Donegal.
He'd gone no further than that,
the radio's battery exhausted by the lies,
nobody on board.

mute

so who would you have called
if the terrible corrections and cries
from the other side
of the plaster and lath
of the bedroom wall
just stopped dead one night

the night it snowed
and we stayed in bed
the following day and watched it snow
just the wall between us
eyes level with the silting sills
back to back in the fraying city
footsole to footsole
as the roads went vacant deadpan
all of them
the rails grew famished and were lost
the buoys in the bay
all motionless on a mute sea?

lunar

London has its own moon
light enough
for the solar-powered ferry on the Serpentine
to tug at its mooring rope at midnight

and hot enough
for the red-haired pale skinned skipper
to strip off her shirt and slip the rope loose

Swimming

I've walked through a door
into the empty warehouse of the sea,
not out of my depth
but nearly.
I have a potter's hands,
limbs that move dreamily.

Now I'm dancing
like an elephant in love
a horse in free-fall
my tattoos sharkskin
hands blue
the shoreline

very far and few.

coastal

here s where the land
frays into shingle,

where the sea s pulse gets
obsessive and there s

almost nothing
for your feet to push against

so each step s a slow
analysis of a step

and you remember
how the processions

always finish in confusion,
how this coastal town s

only home for a while,
its pearly sea-mists

spoiled by dusk
like blood tick-ticking

into a proffered saucer
of bread and milk

Citizen

I have ended up in a sea-side town
full of old people, paused,
on balconies
like photographs in open drawers.

Once, I belonged to The Party,
holidayed in Romania with Progress Tours,
and refused to sign the visitors' book
in The People's Museum.
(Coffee was diabolical.
Stamps on postcards home wouldn't stick.)

Now leaflets, red and blue,
have appeared overnight on my doormat
and I feel more at a loss than I was
and sometimes my mouth is full of coffee
or my eyes full of water
and I have no memory of having lifted
or put down any cup
or thought at all.

Bournemouth

The kids leaving Bliss were shivering in flimsy skirts and shirts, the cold bleaching the skin on their faces as the rain pattered dismally on the roofs of cars sluicing by on... street. It was four in the morning, the moon's candle nearly burnt out.

And I walked
through the middle of town
to St Peter's church
and saw how the fine form of man had become
the mortal remains of Mary Shelley
author of Frankenstein
and *the heart of her husband Percy Byshe Shelley*
degraded and wasted *Poet*

how the corruption of death
had succeeded to the blooming cheek of life
how the worm had inherited the mould
around the grave
drawn out suddenly like a wriggling soul
into the space of heaven
by the wonders of the eye and brain and beak
of the robin

and I sprayed
blood is the price of petrol
on the church door
the solvent spores fresh on the air
the beacon on the crossing outside *Habitat*
pulsing pale sulphur

Antarctica

But this house

when the lights come on
and the windows melt

and my family move
through warm air

under the combed roof
as if we might

(or someone else)
remain

with the house gone
the land changed

the moon patched up
and pitched again

a candle-lit tent
on a raft of ice

among star-stains
on a breathing sea

Robin

In the very
beginning. Imagine.
First light

with no *where* to fall.
An economy of gifts.
And here,

on a twig
of gorse
this robin

alights.

rainstorm with goldfish

a low-voltage apricot glow
deep under the burst glaze
of the surface
drifting
up through fresh reoxygenated water
to gaze
at the apocryphal world
tangerine and amazed

beach road

in the way once
sleep would come

an oystercatcher

up
into its wings

opening just
as we closed our eyes

steps

Surfer in Autumn

A hooded man
watches from the railings;
a woman crouches
out of the wind.

Tar-dipped
and hard to see,
their surfer is prone,
head-on to the swell,

where he spins
and paddles,
half-stands and falls.

≈

How short the day is
that he turns back towards,
ankle-deep, knee-deep
dragging his board,
now the audience has gone.
And his hands are trembling
as if they held birds.

The Spiders

It was cold outside
and the big spiders
were drifting in.

There was one
in the slippery
crucible of the bath.

I lifted it up,
carefully in a cup,
to float it

again,
without joy or regret,
on the intricate

shallows of its legs.

breaking the silence

back of the pond
in the early dark
thinning a stand of
fishing-pole bamboo
(*Phyllostachys*...
somethingorother)
I kneel exhausted
to gather cut canes

≈

a tiny frog's
out on the water
perched on a feather
sage creature
bruised thumbnail
adrift between
the fixed
and the swimming stars

morning song

there was a frog
memorized
under ice

and a bird-skull
beached
on the palm of my hand

little perched ghost
go-between
empty tent

now I steal
disturbed
through eye-holes airways

fontanelles clearings
and the flock
lifts from the wood

the bone skiff
of the beak floats

on a song
you'd shrink

from singing

Cows

after Edwin Muir

Our life is changed; their coming our beginning.

Long after they'd made their covenant with silence,
and the horses had gone,
our mother told us the story of the cows.

How she'd seen them in the valley,
strange as moraine. *Their size!
How self-contained they were!*

And how the whole herd turned,
as if they'd smelled our thoughts.
And galumphed away, all of them,

cows and calves,
along the valley,
across the surface of the earth

faster and faster,
*until their hooves were suddenly
just parading on air*

*their softly mooing bodies
those clouds.*

Dying Dog

Loose straw
with currants for eyes.
She's wild again
and will not come to her name.

Near the Pole

Nothing rots at the earth's end:
a frozen dog with glassy hair,
an outpost full of blown snow.
I dig it out to recall what's there.

On the dining table a copy of *The Field*
dated, May 1904,
More rain than is suitable for this time of year.
A novel by Conan-Doyle on the floor.

And here a row of biscuit tins
across the room on a piece of cord.
Imagine them all limbo dancing,
officers and men, into the unexplored.

Bunuel's Unmade Film

A mouth says, *Go!* and the priests begin.
They say Mass as fast as they can,
making signs of the cross and reaching the most
incredible speeds,
as some of the older priests
stagger,
like boxers,
and turn to the congregation
for the Dominus Vobiscum,
everyone standing and kneeling,
standing and kneeling
as babies shriek and
children laugh and
the altar boys hustle
back and forth
with the missal and other
ritual objects.
Until the mouth says,
Stop! Stop!

And following a pause,
having said the mass in
less than a minute (a record),

Father Donal O'Donal
of Kildare in County Kildare accepts
the prize of a monstrance,
which he kisses
and balances on his head for the photographs.

Book with ants and a fly

Ants cross the page of the abandoned book
(*Don Quixote* again!)

wood ants, I think, *Formica Rufa?*
like rain on snow or

consonants blown loose
from the peg of a vowel.

So many, many books...
But watch them, my ruffians,

spook
that poised librarian,

at the top of the page,
Musa Domestica,

the great sphinx fly!

Car Wash

Car wash sah?
You avoid the face.
Ragged trousers, flared and frayed,
dragging in the oily dust;
bare feet, black skinned,
soles as pink as under scabs.

I wanted to leave him well behind
but a fingerprint stayed just
beyond the edge of the wiper's arc,
beyond our counterfeit exchange.
A watermark.

Second Hand Cadillac

Cadillac, Cadillac, long and dark, shiny and black...

Cocaine bought an Eldorado Sedan,
with two good tires and a drive-train problem
for Jean-Baptiste, our barefoot Haitian,
the condominium's
sleepy night-watchman.
(Just a pinch ripped-off
from the planeloads Floridians glutted on.)

≈

Later that day he was hung by the neck
from a mangrove tree
bare feet stretching
to be tickled by the waves

leaving the Cadillac dumped junk,
there still at the edge of the lot
if you look
where the scrub was cut
and's now grown back.

Shanty Town

It was a cheap country
and we could afford to tip
the bus-boy a tenner
by mistake
in the Sheraton
with its marble bathrooms
and open-air
roof-top pool
like a blue silk flower.

Late at night
on a cable channel
parachuting naked girls
came floating by
like magnified seeds
and our currency ripened
and began to smell
under the immense pillows.

Ex-Patriots

On our last morning we take coca-tea early
in *Confiteria Elis*
on the *Avenue of the Sixteenth of July*.
The thin air of a high altitude dawn
and the peeled light make the world seem new.

Ayamaras from Tiahuanaco
are arriving for the market on Avenue Bolivar.
An unsophisticated people,
whose ancestors were found
living among ruins they could no longer explain.

They have bags full of chickens,
foetal llamas, squealing piglets,
simmering buckets of creamy grubs.

≈

Last night our sleep was disturbed again.
With the full moon's rising
a drug plane came in low over the trees
to the south of Marsh Harbour.
There was the drone on and on of an unlit boat
somewhere between Salt Cay and the horizon.

On the Shining Path

They took Guzman alive
in a Lima suburb,
desirable, detached residence.
The perfect disguise.

He'd been unseen for years so
people were whispering:
He never existed.
He's my brother-in-law.
I loved him once.

But here he is, hauled from his bed
out to the cameras
and alive all right.
Those poor, sagging old-man's breasts.
Puta madre!
Asesino!

Oxford Town

after Brecht

A student gives
the last slice of his pizza
to a beggar
and a man who was hungry
is less so.
(Although the world isn't changed by this.)

One stranger gives
the last slice of a pizza
to another,
the world
isn't changed by this,
(although someone who was hungry
is less so).

Freetown

Nights when the moon was sunk without trace
the unlit planes would ghost in low over coral
where the sea teethed and worried the lagoon.

We took a Jeep out once beyond the last
of the guard-dogged, half-built houses
to where the only road just petered

out but kept on driving through the trees
to Freetown's roofless, peeling shacks,
rotten, upturned boats on a littered shore.

Then further out to where the crashed planes were:
scattered like jacks around a still clearing,
Dakotas and Cessnas slewed and ditched,

and right in the middle a pool:
deep and oblong, blown from the rock
with a springboard and silver ladders.

The water was fresh and the palest blue
over white coral like air
lapping at a nest's edge.

undertow

we were real
the sand logged the weight of us both

my foot-prints deep at the heel
hers faint fossils

    ≈

we undressed and swam
testicles and breasts

peculiarly light
as the wind picked up

and whitened the waves

driving in snow

from the night
white bee-ghosts come
and fly against the fragile glass

asleep in the seat-belt next to me
your dark shape is
waiting summer

kate's feet

massaging oil into your tired feet
I trace the arch that takes the weight of you

a dream of bones in a clear foot breaking
wings panting like a fish's gills in the air

I wake up sweaty and watch you breathing
float my hand in your atmosphere of hair

whales

in our attic of glass
she kicks off the covers
and we sprawl among stars

naked as whales
huge and graceful and slow
tender and tiny in the southern oceans

taking a bath

four in the morning just after the birth
the house is as still as the earth

I undress slowly to sustained applause
from the helpless taps *It was nothing please*

then step down into water that is like
a simple amoeba of light

Party

In late August
the flat roof-top was
slightly tacky,
everyone's dancing slowed down.

So you're the poet!
we heard one dancer
yell to another,
embarrassed by silence

as the music stopped
and your breast-milk bloomed
suddenly through silk
into dark rosettes.

Child

This is a poor place
to offer you to sleep,
ridged and hard,
all sinew and collar-bone,
with the clip-clop of my coconut heart.
But you accept it,
lay your cheek against the stain of my breast
and stop crying.

≈

Home late,
hardly knowing my own hands,
I levered you up to my chest
and recognised your weight,
your breathing against the side of my neck,
my own lightness
held by you.

Definitions

There was a word game we were playing
with friends and their children:
strange, abandoned words
you had to invent definitions for.
And Isaac was excited
because he'd written a great one.
Can you read it? he said.
Can you read it Dad?

And I could, almost,
a rare and beautiful cloth.........
but the last few words were scrawled and lost.

He snatched the words back.
Slammed the door.

Was asleep when I found him,
paper still gripped in his hand.
I slipped it loose and worked out the scrawl,
then closed the curtains
on fleet clouds
and a dragonfly moon.

As I do again now,
the child grown and the word long forgotten,
for his *rare and beautiful cloth
made of silk and quartz.*

The Lecture

John Clare I forgive you
all the snoring and the crying
out in your sleep.

You weren't alone, it was
so warm after lunch.
I could hear myself

stumbling as I lectured
at my lectern and you'd come
more than a hundred years

to hear me mess with your words:
your *Nightingale,* your *Clock-a-Clay,*
your *Mary*....

≈

Now in the night, in my bed
I can't sleep, I can't
escape from words

and my son wakes,
third night in a row,
with the terrors of the dark upon him,

eyes open
but in another world,
stumbling in.

≈

I would take his terrors if I could.
But they are not mine, will not become words,

so he huddles at my side,
cold and frightened, learning to be alone

and all I can do, John Clare, John Clare,
is take his hand and stroke his hair

on the long walk home.

The Neon Party

I'm waiting outside a village hall
to collect you from a party.
It's the early hours and I'm alone.

There's a crumb-trail of mist
along a river,
snow in the headlights of a passing car.

And it comes to me again
how far out in the land we are
how narrow and winding and

easily effaced the roads
how late it is
and how little I know of your friends
or mine.

Lullaby

for K and I

Sleep now boys and the snow will fall.
And you'll wake, god willing,
among roses and cloves,
your footprints waiting
at the edge of the trees

with the deer-slot, cat's paw,
the sparrow's
hieroglyph,
here
        and there,

as if
as if

human cat bird deer
might have stood once
or in time to come
in the deep cold
close together

The Possibility of Snow

The pages of the snow-fall
are opening, they flicker
and the little
derelict school
shivers.

Back of the playground
nettles stir
over lost things:
milk-teeth, footballs,

and the sticky lens
tweezered from the jelly
of a sheep's eye,
surprise

of finding our
own world there
but upside down
now blurred, now sharp

and the spaces
inside a rabbit's heart
we opened carefully
like a hymn book
with tiny knives.

Hate

You're sixteen and just beginning
to hate yourself.

You can't know why.
It's the springtime perhaps:

its piercing showers,
its roads scattered

with rabbits and squirrels
hedgehogs and birds

eyeless in tangled robes
of skin and feathers and fur.

Or just a door slamming
at four a.m.

as someone comes
or someone goes.

But it's hate you wake to. Hate.
A homeless feeling

on the far side of the earth from love.

Leveret

I cycled past it no-handed
on the way to school

a leveret in the gutter
cuddling its own guts

and when I couldn't sleep
I'd cup

the weight
of my genitals

in my hands
my acorns my lamb's heart

Conjuring Rowena

See Martin and Jonathan, David and John,
unspooling a burning
ribbon of magnesium
through the spinney, into the dark,

their path waning,
to a trace of her name
written in the air,
an afterglow,

of phosphorescence and spoor,
a whiff of witchery
deep among trees,
where they speak

of *Rowena*, still
Rowena, spelling
her name into theirs,
(*Rowena Edwards! Johnathan Mead!*)

Dream-body and flesh.
Such shamelessness
on that wedding night
in that scald of light.

But Don't look at it!
Don't look!

≈

Now the magnesium's done,
the spinney built on

(none of us blind)
although Jonathan's bones

are lights in the river.
30 years dead.

And Rowena? who knows
about her now or remembers

that retinal trace
the sting, the letters re-

versed on the backs of our eyes
a collap-

sing star
a new

order, constellations
rising, the burning

boys setting out
from a spinney

for strange homes?

Grand Canyon

for Ian

We'd started down in the late afternoon
and a Mormon ranger

was asking some smokers
to guess how long

a cigarette-butt
might last in the desert.

*Your President's
a cunt,* I said so they heard.

It was thousands
of years, we wore

red bandanas
and didn't smoke.

Leave no trace he was saying.
It was Reagan

just staring at us
in that way he had

all quizzical and so
democratically bemused

like a footprint on the moon
I thought

Jain monks? I said
to a girl the River

Colorado was invisible
and enormous

like America
or evolution

the office
of the president

his bomb.

Jesus!
The way she looked at me.

So weird.
Like the future.

Delinquents

for M, J and P

In hushed single-file I'm leading my brothers
along the side of the house
past the after-lunch Welsh of our garrulous uncles
being sieved into fine *yakedada*
by the meshed aperture that keeps the pantry cool.

We're heading for the room that's kept for Sundays
and the newly dead
with its perfect cushions, its fruit withheld
in shelved cut glass, the astounding
Stereogram!
with a jewelled eye that greens
and deepens when you switch it on.

How I poked out that eye
with a pencil sharpened
precisely for the job
and led my brothers
undiscovered away;

how we stole an orange
peeled it and shared it
equally, by touch
in the citrus-scented
darkness of our bedroom
is a story I tell
more and more often
to myself now.

Frank O'Hara's Collected Poems

It's the same edition: *Vintage Books,*
with the cover collage by Larry Rivers,
never published in Britain;

the one I lifted from Bowes and Bowes
years ago when I was almost young,
tucked under my vest

under my ex-US-army jacket,
which had pockets inside pockets,
all empty save for some tiny and

mysterious deposits of sand,
that were there when I bought it,
that made me think

of shorelines and beaches:
Fire Island, the Bay of Pigs,
Juno and Gold, Castro

landing at Las Coloradas,
that I grind
between fingertips

for courage
as I wait.
As I grow old.

Homesick Blues

I don't believe you... You're a liar!
Bob Dylan

Last time I saw Mitch, Spring of '83,
he was in love and happy.
Now news from home of *Kerb-Crawling Pests!*
and his shamed mugshot in the local press.

So I play Subterranean Homesick Blues,
first time in years.
Fucking loud! he'd have said with a smile,
cicadas so noisy hear I can barely here.

But there's the petrol smell still
of his Tiger-Cub to go on,
drip of its crankcase oil onto grass,
ticking down through the half-lives of memory,

until born again and barely credible,
slouching across the miles-away stage,
here's Dylan himself,
us rapt, just watching him lift his guitar,

carefully, as if road grit
stung still under the skin of his palms.

Grandfather/Clock

It's actually quite a simple mechanism,
says Dad, looking in
at the workings. Like all
mechanisms
in my experience,
it is
and it isn't.

(Time passes)

During which we fail
to get the clock to tick
or tock and drift

back
to the old, old tale
of *Great-Granddad's Tackle!*
scalped in Somme-forests
by a shrapnel-flake
his pendulum
and weights
down there in the mud
stump among stumps, all
of his mechanism.

But *Look!* Dad's saying,
I remember it breaking.
That's the old man's print!

(It's right there in the putty
holding clock-face glass.)

And across eighty years,
we lift
our prints
to that print
and touch.

What ratio
of Duty/Respect/Curiosity/Love
sends men to war or brings them to touch?
I'm thinking later
as I get undressed in the room I slept in
through unfathomable adolescence,
and looking down notice
a perfectly white pubic hair,
frost-thread,
wayward spring,
child lost in a dark forest,
my first.

Erosion

The cliff-top bench where I sat one evening
years ago, with my oldest friend and the poet, Sweeney,
dedicated to the memory of Roger and Joan (*they were happiest here*)
has vanished. It's lodged about 20 feet down

at an awkward angle among rocks and earth.
Are you happy now Roger! Sweeney might have said
and he'd have been interested to be sure
in the rumours of vagrants

entombed in the buried beach-huts below.
Because he was famous for that sort of thing I suppose
in the way some poets or friends from childhood
are famous, which is to say not really at all,

despite talk of revivals, promises of phone-calls.
But seeing them in the park that morning was a shock.
Arm in arm singing, *This Charming Man.*
My friend and Sweeney. Had they purposed to avoid me?

Or was Sweeney just doing what poets do:
missing trains and corrupting the young?
I should have asked. I could have done.
But we were rounding up students: *Poetry! Litrechewer!*

So I gave them signed copies of my *Coconut Heart*
instead, when they left.(*available online*)
and a kind commuter posted one back to me,
(via the publisher)

along with some copies of her own poems,
from Waterloo where she'd found it dropped.
Or left. (The station not the site
of the battle, the suffering, the actual, bloody agony.)

Unreal!

Only a cock stood on the rooftree
Co co rico co co rico!
TS Eliot

Storm the studios of reality
re-take the universe!

in pale blue chalk,
top corner of the blackboard
in the seminar room.

Had he chalked it there,
our Professor Philips
with his tedious beard, his

Whole Earth Catalogue,
snot-green corduroys
and non-descript hair?

He'd have needed a chair.
Although he knew by heart
What the Thunder Said,

and took a shot once
at reciting it:

(You'd have sniggered too
at his eyes-closed, nasal, oddly
stressed, self-
deprecating *co co rico!*)

But what did we know?
At nineteen!
We should have listened.

This morning before dawn
on my fortieth birthday,
I remembered him.

A cockerel was crowing
on another island, some distance away
across the wine-dark sea,

for no one and nothing.

Saint Martin

Flat on my back
in a hospital bed
in my 50th year
under a thin sheet
in the indirect
northerly light
of a February morning,
I'm a sketch of shadows
like the brass-rubbing
from St Martin's church
that hung on the landing
(cold stone
stained glass)
my mother's voice
explaining once again
to her dreamy,
forgetful,
tender-hearted child
who this was.

Something

I have something to tell you
my mother said.
We were all together in a room
at the far end of summer.
She seemed sad and happy.
I felt very young.
I was trying not to think
about the obvious things
but couldn't help noticing
the darkness thickening
more quickly
inside than out.
And how no one had pulled the curtains
with their abstract motif
which always reminded me
of boats: nightfishermen
in a becalmed flotilla
launched each night
on waves of soft cotton.
I can see
her face.
It is soft stone.
Her lowered eye-lids are veined marble.
Her hair white over grey.
But more like an unfledged bird
or something
than anything old.

Nativity

My father hadn't thought it possible.
During the night,
after the calves were taken,
the cows had jumped or broken through
every fence, hedge and padlocked gate.

And in the morning were standing
outside the barn bellowing,

while the discreet midwife
made her way downstairs
and people in the village
set off for work
in cars and on bicycles.

As usual.
As necessary.

Mother to Child

Your father is worried about you.
He avoids hot baths,
wears saggy underpants,
walks like John Wayne
in *The Undefeated*
as if his testicles were egg-yolks
in cobweb slings.

He grows angry sometimes
for his starving continents of sperm,
my empty-stomach pain.
You'd have been ugly anyway, he thinks,
or stupid. I know he does.

But you're perfect,
I insist,
like my own childhood,
our early love,
or this huge, distorted harvest-moon
that night after night doesn't wane.

The Great Umbrella

My son's awake, upset
and I pause on the stairs
to listen to his mother

telling him to imagine
a perfect, empty beach
and a great umbrella there

under which all the people he loves
are sitting.
He names them,

as I do,
Jim and Mae and Eve and Sue...
the warm waves combing

each over each:
Sue's well,

*under the umbrella
isn't she?*
Voice nearly free

of his sleepy body.
*Well under,
my darling, yes.*

Leeks

My brother rises to the surface of the uncurtained window
bringing leeks just pulled from the dark garden.

In the living room his wife's asleep in a chair.
He grips the blue-grey of the leaves,

pauses to stare at the window's black.
Our faces are shocked eye-whites.

There is nothing that can help her.

Undertakers

On the hot pavement
one man widens

another's eye
with his fingers

looking for a cinder
or a dust grain.

While I'm hoping
that death

might look like sleep.
But it doesn't

not at all.

grief

for Jim

your eyes and nose and mouth
were points

in a pattern of stars undone
by a blink

all the palaces of your voice
the labyrinths of your fingerprints

West Ogwell Church Devon, March 2019

Kathrin Harris is buried here
The Beloved daughter of John and Anne
Of Moulton Northamptonshire.

She died in this Parish at the residence of her Sister,
March 30th 1870,
In her Seventeenth year.

Also Anne, Mother of the above,
Aged 76 (though the date's unclear.
1 March 1896?)

Yes. Both in March, this month,
All the early lambs
Calling in the fields:

Mère!... Maaa!...
As they must have then
On both March days.

I promise you

Martin! you'll barely even notice the sky shutting down its tender autumnal friction-burns of oranges and lemon-yellows and reds and all the shapes of darkness behind lips and the skin under your fingernails white as spilled milk on this pavement you've walked so many times thinking about work those corner-shops you knew as a child liquorice thefts corpse-dust in the gutters of the paths to the church or awake in the dark on that island where you lived just after you were married imagining
the houses we'd live in in the days to come the children we'd have and their names who'd be better than us in our ordinary lives walking home from those corner shops grown thinner thinking about work and things and how the boys are doing now all of us alone grown up both of them all of us yes oranges and lemons on the trees then and still so far from home

sweeping the monastery porch cittaviveka

a wood-pigeon flops down
(*drops heavily/fails*)
onto a patch of sunlight

stirring up a great
cloud-of-dust
and just

sits there
as the dust
settles

through sunlight
a wood-pigeon
just that

but splendid
(*magnificent/splendiferous/glorious/
excellent*)

yes
that's right
in a bright cloud

Ash

A week or so later
rain-drops
at an ash-tree's
branch-tips
find
the whole of the light
and you can watch
if you like
how the daughters
(for the most part
quiet
some laughter
moving hands
whispering lips)
lift
each image up
from boxes and boxes
of beaches and gardens
nieces and nephews
cousins and uncles and aunts
to pencil
mother as a child
mother in London
mother married
mother old
on the backs of photographs
they set apart.

Allotment

After weeks without rain the top-soil shattered
and sizzled inauspiciously away from the spade
in the dry wind.

I assumed some control,
placing seed at the right depth,
with the right gap between rows.

Nothing!
So out there planting at full-moon
muttering spells.

Still nothing showed, but
we began to notice
other things:

driving to work
the pleasing conjunction
of EGGS/LOGS on a sign by the road,

and a sail moving across a field
in the shy distances
meaning water.

River in the Woods

First light and a river in the woods
float me half-awake
watersmeet
sweetchestnut
sessile oak

kate? I say sleepily
kate?
again *kate?*

until you murmur
and turn to me
and your name's
weight settles
in a cot of branches
above the flood.

≈

Listen.
There will be purple scabious
this morning kate
outside our bedroom window
broom and violets
salvia and rosemary.

balcony

where I waited
and wait

for you to come home
old man martin

old woman kate
hushed stadium

of stars and leaves
endless

in-breath of the city

The Rest of My Life

Although he do not dress like the other teachers he still is a good teacher. He said he don't like beating because he wouldn't like if people beat him. Mr Edwards is tall he has black eyes and a huge head. He has long fingers with a lought of hair. Mr Edwards likes to say good things to people and always says thanks. He likes to say pleas too.
Cornelius Henfield (12)

30 years ago or so today, (*7 April 1989*)
first lesson of the morning
in a tin-roofed classroom
(*8 Mile Rock Government High, Freeport, Grand Bahama*)
while I was thinking about
who knows what
we think about,
(*Tennis with Peter? Snorkelling with Kate?*)
certainly, how I'd hate
for the rest of my, (*Life?*)
to do, you know..,
(*Teach!*)
Cornelius Henfield (12)
was writing that.
Which has turned up here
(*And now*) on my last day of teaching
in a pile of old books
I was about to chuck out.
And he'd be old now too,
Cornelius, as we are, (*Were!*)
Martin and Peter and Kate,
Ilone and Steve...
(*And everyone else I hope*)
but it's all gone well
in general
maybe (*For him/you?*)
as it does.

We're alive! (*Or were*)
At least. (*You are!*)
And I've not forgotten my manners.
And I've never been or had
beaten anyone yet.
(*A huge head still!*)
With the black eyes
stuck to it? (*Weirdo!*)
Although,
I'll tell you
(*I'll tell you Cornelius...*)
one extraordinary thing:
(*Says the man who shaves his fingers still!*)
Sorry, listen, just listen...
oh... but bless you Cornelius anyway.
(*Whoever you were/are*)
Where was I?
(*We*) Forgive me everyone please
whatever we were thinking
about then,
the tennis and the snorkelling.
(*Just ordinary kindness?*)
Yes.
In the morning of our lives,
longago now.

In 1989

our hammocks still swing
in the evening shadows
of sea-grape trees

as The Wall comes down
and the harbour approaches
unfurl into kite-tails

of navigation lights
on Mandela's release.
We believe

absolutely
in Politics
and that a self might be

lulled open and changed
between morning and morning,
as the night-ferry,

slows and sways
on the swell,
slipping

away to the out-islands,
prodigal at the bow-rail
flipping a fag-end

like a comet.

White Moths

Give my love to oh... anybody

what wakes here
in the hermitage and the rookery

out of all apparent time and place
in this absolute dark

before we start
by the dawn's early light?

(or *cold!*)

Up now though and standing,
all of us,

loved or waiting,
feathers in the darkness,

candle at the glass,
behind all these eyes,

these unlatched gates into morning.

Acknowledgements

Some of these poems first appeared in *Brittle Star, The Frogmore Papers, The Interpreter's House, Iron, London Magazine, Navis, The North, Obsessed with Pipework, Poetry and Audience, Smith's Knoll, The Red Wheelbarrow, The Rialto* and *Stand*. Thanks to the editors.

A number of these poems, or versions of them, were published in the pamphlets *Coconut Heart* (Redbeck Press) and *Rainstorm with Goldfish* (Happenstance).

I owe a debt of gratitude to Don Atkinson and Kate Edwards for their encouragement and inspiration and for reading and commenting on earlier versions of this collection.